The 5 W's of Transforming Your Life: Why, What, Where, When, and Who

Roseanne Nyoike

Published by Roseanne Nyoike, 2024.

While every precaution has been taken in the preparation of this book, the publisher assumes no responsibility for errors or omissions, or for damages resulting from the use of the information contained herein.

THE 5 W'S OF TRANSFORMING YOUR LIFE: WHY, WHAT, WHERE, WHEN, AND WHO

First edition. December 4, 2024.

ISBN: 979-8230903390

Written by Roseanne Nyoike.

To my sister Lydia,

For your unwavering love and care, as a devoted mother, a wonderful auntie, and a steadfast friend.Despite the demands of your life as a teacher, you give selflessly, balancing every role with grace, strength, and an open heart. Your dedication inspires and your kindness lights up our lives.

With love and gratitude, this is for you.

'In the rush of life, it's not the roles we juggle, but the love we pour into them that truly defines us.'

Introduction

The 5 W's of Transforming Your Life:

Why, What, Where, When, and Who

A practical self-help guide that helps readers reflect on and answer the key questions needed to reshape their lives. Using the 5 W's, the Why, What, Where, When, and Who. This book guides readers through a journey of self-discovery, goal setting and meaningful change.

WHY: Discover Your Purpose

Why do you feel stuck or unfulfilled?

Why do your goals matter to you?

Exercises to dig deep and uncover the 'why' behind your dreams and desires.

WHAT: Define Your Goals

What do you truly want in life personally, professionally, emotionally?

What steps can you take to get closer to your vision?

Tips for setting achievable, actionable goals and overcoming fear of failure.

WHERE: Create the Right Environment

Where are you now physically, mentally, emotionally and is it serving you?

Where do you need to be to thrive?

Guidance on building environments that support growth, from relationships to physical spaces.

WHEN: Take Action at the Right Time

When is the right time to make a change?

How to recognize procrastination and seize opportunities

Strategies to create timelines, set priorities, and develop patience when results take time.

WHO: Build Your Support System

Who do you need in your life to help you succeed?

How to foster meaningful relationships and let go of toxic connections.

Identifying mentors, partners, and a community that aligns with your goals.

Chapter 1: WHY: Discover Your Purpose

Your purpose in life is to find your purpose and give your whole heart and soul to it.’

– Buddha

Many of us move through life on autopilot following paths dictated by society, family or circumstance. But true transformation begins when you identify your ‘why’. This is your inner purpose, your reason for getting out of bed in the morning and the force that drives your dreams. Without a clear ‘why’ even the best plans can feel hollow.

Rachel’s Story: Rediscovering Her Why

Rachel had always envisioned a life of diplomacy and global impact. For 12 years, she thrived in her role with the United Nations, working on humanitarian projects across Africa. It was the career she had dreamed of

since college and a career that allowed her to travel, make meaningful contributions, and connect with diverse cultures. But when her department faced budget cuts, Rachel’s position was unexpectedly eliminated.

At 39, with two young children enrolled in one of Kenya’s most prestigious international schools, Rachel faced a stark reality. She had no backup plan. Her savings wouldn’t last forever, and the school fees were extremely high. When she learned the school offered an 85% fee discount for staff, Rachel reluctantly signed up for a two-year teaching course.

Getting a teaching job right after graduating was an incredible opportunity and it gave her the sense of accomplishment she had been striving for. However, becoming a middle school teacher was not part of the dream she had envisioned for herself. Despite this detour from her original plan, the position turned out to be more than just a job; it became a much needed lifeline. It offered her stability during uncertain times, a

chance to grow professionally and a way to make a meaningful impact on young minds.

Rachel's first few years in the classroom were anything but smooth. Teaching middle school students in a high achieving environment came with its own set of challenges. The students were sharp, outspoken and constantly testing boundaries. Rachel had the knowledge and skills to design engaging lessons, but classroom management was another story. Each day felt like a battle to maintain order while fostering creativity and critical thinking.

The chaos of group projects overwhelmed her, especially when the activities required taking students outside the classroom to explore concepts in a more hands-on way. Keeping everyone on task in these less structured settings proved to be a constant challenge.

Mediating arguments, ensuring progress and managing distractions added to her workload. Grading their work afterward meant spending late nights poring over assignments, only to face complaints from parents whose children struggled with the tasks or did not perform well, making her feel as though her efforts were underappreciated.

Parent-teacher conferences became her least favorite part of the job. The parents at this prestigious international school were not only paying exorbitant tuition fees but also expected premium service for their money. They dissected her every teaching method, questioned her discipline decisions and even criticized trivial matters like the choice of seating arrangements.

One parent famously demanded a meeting because Rachel had not responded to their email within 24 hours. Another insisted she redo a project rubric because their child claimed it was 'confusing.'

The pressure was not just from the students and their parents. The school's management operated like a high end business catering to elite clientele. The school

prided itself on being one of the best international institutions in Kenya, attracting the children of diplomats, business moguls, and celebrities. This reputation came with high expectations for teachers like Rachel.

Academic performance was just one piece of the puzzle. The school offered an extensive range of extracurricular activities from environmental clubs to pantomime productions and sports teams to debate clubs all of which required teacher involvement.

Rachel found herself stretched thin, coaching after-school debate sessions and supervising weekend sports fixtures.

While the school day officially ended in the early afternoon, Rachel's work rarely did. Her mornings began before sunrise as she prepared lessons and dropped off her kids. Evenings were consumed by grading, lesson planning and emails. Weekends, which she had hoped to reserve for her family, were frequently hijacked by school tournaments and sometimes training.

The school administration evaluated teachers not only on student performance but also on how satisfied parents were. A single negative review could lead to

lengthy meetings and pressure to improve in areas that often felt more about appeasing paying clients than delivering meaningful education.

Rachel knew she was earning significantly more than government teachers but the salary came at a steep price. Every day felt like she was trading her energy,

creativity and peace of mind for financial stability. The once practical benefits of the job were her children's reduced fees and the aligned holidays began to feel like handcuffs.

She felt like she was constantly on the clock, her time no longer her own. Even her family noticed. Her children, while grateful for the time spent together during commutes, missed the more relaxed version of their mom who used to play board games or tell bedtime stories.

Rachel began to ask herself hard questions: Is this sustainable? Is this worth it? Can I keep doing this for another year or five?

Despite the challenges, Rachel did her best to adjust. She learned how to handle difficult parents with calm professionalism, deflecting their criticisms with firm but polite responses. She developed a better rhythm for grading and planning, often setting time limits for tasks to avoid burnout.

But the truth remained, she was enduring the job, not enjoying it. Even as she gained confidence in the classroom, she struggled to find fulfillment. Teaching was simply a means to an end and the longer she stayed the more disconnected she felt from herself.

But as she thought of her life then, the benefits outweighed the struggle. She could drop her kids off at school, teach in the same building and drive home with them. School holidays aligned perfectly, allowing her to spend quality time with her children without the guilt of work commitments. The fee discount was a financial lifesaver. For Rachel, teaching was not a passion, it was a practical solution.

Rachel's routine became increasingly unsustainable. The relentless demands from parents, management, and extracurricular obligations drained her energy and eroded her patience. Her breaking point came one rainy Saturday during a school-wide athletics tournament, an event where the school spared no expense. Management had hired an elite stadium to host the event, bringing together students from their branches across the country. It was meant to be a grand showcase of the institution's excellence.

But the weather had other plans.

It rained cats and dogs that day, turning the pristine stadium into a soggy, chaotic mess. The event was eventually canceled, but not before Rachel found herself in the downpour, frantically trying to shepherd groups of drenched, shivering kids onto buses. Chaos reigned as students complained about ruined uniforms and cold fingers, while irate parents called her phone demanding updates on the situation.

Rachel was soaked to the bone, her umbrella rendered useless against the heavy rain and wind. She helped load sports equipment and consoled tearful children who had looked forward to the event for weeks. The management, safely sheltered back in school barked orders at her and other teachers over the phone. By the time she finally got onto a bus herself, she was physically and emotionally drained.

The rainstorm was not the end of Rachel's ordeal. By the time she got home that evening, she was chilled and aching. The next morning, she woke up with a fever, a sore throat, and a pounding headache. She could barely get out of bed but the school management began calling her incessantly to check when she would return to work. And even though she was sick, she was expected to send emails to cover all her lessons while she was out.

Despite her condition, Rachel dragged herself to her laptop to prepare lesson plans and worksheets for her classes. She answered a steady stream of emails from colleagues and the administration, who seemed oblivious to her struggle. At one point her eldest child who was also sick gently took her laptop away, insisting she rest. But Rachel knew she could not afford to neglect her responsibilities, not when the school treated every absence as an inconvenience.

For three days, she battled her illness while juggling work from her bed. The fever broke eventually, but the experience left her utterly exhausted and emotionally frayed.

Lying in bed on the third night of her illness, Rachel stared at the ceiling and thought, what am I doing? She had pushed herself to the brink for a job that seemed to care more about its reputation and profit

margins than the well-being of its staff. She thought about the endless parent complaints, the after school activities, and now the expectation that she would continue working even when sick.

For the first time, Rachel admitted to herself that she could not keep going like this. She had joined teaching out of necessity, not passion. But now, even the practicality of the job which included its salary, benefits, and aligned schedule with her children felt insufficient to justify the toll it was taking on her body and spirit.

As Rachel recovered from her illness, she found herself taking stock of her life. The fever-induced haze had lifted, but the deeper fatigue remained with a weariness that came from years of neglecting her own happiness and health. She began to question everything. She asked herself the question 'Why am I really doing this? Is this what I want my life to look like? What example am I setting for my kids?

In the weeks that followed, Rachel began to reflect deeply on her life and her future The answer was not immediate but it sparked a process of reflection that would eventually lead her to rediscover herself

One evening, after tucking her children into bed, Rachel opened a dusty old notebook she had not touched in years. Inside were handwritten pages from her days at the United Nations: reflections on her travels, notes from field visits, and drafts of articles she had once written with pride. As she flipped through the pages, a forgotten spark reignited.

She had loved writing and telling stories that mattered, capturing the voices of people who rarely had a platform. Writing had been her escape, her way of understanding the world and herself.

That night, she wrote for the first time in years. It wasn't perfect or polished, but it was hers. She wrote about the rain-soaked tournament, the frustration of being pulled in every direction, and the aching realization that she had lost sight of herself.

In the weeks that followed, Rachel carved out time for writing. At first, it was just ten minutes before bed or while her kids did their homework. Writing became her outlet, a way to process the challenges of her job and the lingering disappointment of not returning to her diplomatic career.

She started sharing her musings anonymously in online forums for teachers. Her posts, filled with humor and honesty, resonated with educators from all over the world. Comments poured in:

'I thought I was the only one who felt this way!

'Thank you for putting this into words'

'You have inspired me to take a step back and prioritize myself.

The validation was overwhelming. For the first time in years, Rachel felt like she was making a difference which was not by fulfilling someone else's demands, but by sharing her truth.

Encouraged by the responses, Rachel began to expand her writing. She wrote essays about the absurdity of balancing work and family life, about the disconnect between the management's expectations and the reality of teaching, and about her own struggles to rediscover her identity.

One day, she received a message from a former colleague who had read one of her essays. 'You should publish these, 'the message read. Your voice is so relatable and it's what so many of us need to hear.

Rachel dismissed the idea at first, doubting that anyone beyond her small circle would care. But the thought lingered. She started researching publishing options and discovered a world of writers who had turned their experiences into books, blogs, and podcasts.

Rachel decided to take a leap of faith. She compiled her essays and wrote a proposal for a book about her journey as a reluctant teacher and the lessons she had learned along the way. She titled it When the Bell Rings: A Teacher's Journey from Survival to Self-Discovery.

To her amazement, a small independent publisher expressed interest. They loved her raw, candid writing and believed her story would resonate with a wide audience including teachers, parents and anyone struggling to balance practicality with passion.

As Rachel worked on her book, she continued teaching, but with a new perspective. She began to set boundaries, refusing to let the school's demands consume her entirely. She delegated tasks when she could and prioritized her mental and physical health.

Her students noticed the change. 'Ms. Rachel, you seem happier,' one of them said one day. It was true but though her workload had not decreased, she now had something to look forward to beyond the classroom.

Her writing became a lifeline, a source of joy and purpose that transcended the daily grind.

By the time her book was published, Rachel had built a small but loyal following online. Teachers and parents alike praised her for her honesty and humor. Her book became a bestseller in educational circles, sparking conversations about the pressures teachers face and the importance of self-care.

Eventually, Rachel made the difficult decision to leave teaching. Her book's success opened doors to new opportunities in speaking engagements, writing workshops, and even consulting for educational organizations.

Though she had once resented teaching, Rachel realized it had been a stepping stone to rediscovering herself. The challenges she faced in the classroom had shaped her, giving her the resilience and clarity to pursue her passion.

Looking back, Rachel saw her journey not as a detour, but as a necessary path to where she was meant to be. She had turned her struggles into a story that inspired others, proving to herself and her children that it's never too late to change direction and find fulfillment.

Her kids, now grown, often teased her about how she used to grumble about her teaching job. 'If you hadn't been a teacher, Mom, you would not have written the book that changed everything!' they'd say.

Rachel could not argue with that.

Rachel's decision to write her book was driven by a mix of determination and a deep-seated need to break free from a life she had been merely surviving. Teaching had never been her passion; it was something she had done out of necessity, to make ends meet, but it never sparked joy. Every day, she felt like she was simply going through the motions of meeting expectations, facing the classroom, but never truly connecting with what she was doing.

The real 'why' behind her decision was her yearning for something more fulfilling. She wanted to write because it was an outlet for the parts of herself that teaching had never allowed her to explore. The book would be her way of reclaiming control over her life and finally pursuing what truly mattered to her.

While writing a full-length book seemed like a daunting challenge, it was also a way to break free from the monotony of her routine. But even as she felt the pull to create, she was left with questions; Where would she start? How could she capture years of her experiences and her journey from surviving to thriving without losing the essence of what truly mattered? And, most importantly, would anyone care about her story?

The answers were not easy, but she realized that the 'why' was the desire to escape the life she had merely endured and that was enough to fuel her decision to begin.

She started by setting a clear goal; one chapter per month. With her teaching schedule still demanding most of her time, she had to write late at night or during early mornings before her children woke up. On weekends, while her kids played football or worked on school projects, Rachel would sit in the corner of the living room, tapping away on her laptop.

The process was not smooth. Some days, the words flowed effortlessly, but on others, she would stare at her screen for hours with nothing to show for it. Doubts crept in. Was her story worth telling? Would anyone care?

One night, after reading over a particularly emotional chapter about her struggles with parent-teacher conferences, she hesitated to include it. Was she being too vulnerable? Her eldest child noticed her hesitation and asked, 'What's wrong, Mom?'

'I'm not sure this is good enough, Rachel admitted.

Her child smiled and said, but it's your story, and someone out there needs to hear it.

That simple encouragement reignited her confidence.

Rachel soon realized she could not do it all alone. She reached out to an old friend from her days at the United Nations, a journalist who had always admired her way with words. Together, they worked on refining the manuscript. The friend helped her organize her

ideas and gave her honest feedback, pushing her to dig deeper into her emotions and experiences.

To keep herself accountable, Rachel joined an online writing group. Every week, she shared her progress

and received feedback from other aspiring authors. Their stories inspired her, and their friendship kept her motivated during moments of self-doubt.

After nearly a year of late nights, early mornings and countless rewrites, Rachel completed her manuscript. She sent it to a few small publishers, bracing herself for rejections. To her surprise, within weeks, one publisher responded with enthusiasm.

We love your voice, their email read. Your story is both relatable and inspiring. We would like to offer you a contract.

Rachel was stunned. The publisher's team worked with her to polish the manuscript further, design a cover, and market the book. Seeing her name on the cover for the first time brought tears to her eyes.

With the book's release, Rachel's life took on a new rhythm. She still had teaching responsibilities but now juggled book signings, interviews and speaking engagements as well.

Her children were her biggest cheerleaders, often helping her pack books for events or brainstorm ideas for her social media posts. They loved teasing her about her growing fan base, calling her Mom, the famous writer.

However, balancing it all was not easy. There were nights when she felt stretched thin, struggling to meet deadlines while still being present for her kids. But Rachel had learned an important lesson during her teaching years: boundaries.

She created a schedule that prioritized her family first, blocking out time for family dinners, movie nights, and weekend outings. Writing and speaking engagements had their place, but not at the expense of her children.

Rachel's book, When the Bell Rings: A Teacher's Journey from Survival to Self-Discovery, resonated with readers far beyond her expectations. Teachers, parents, and even students wrote to her, sharing how her story had inspired them.

Her success also had an unexpected impact on her children. Watching their mother pursue her dreams taught them invaluable lessons about resilience, self-belief, and the importance of following one's passion even if the path to it was not straightforward.

One evening, her youngest child asked, 'Mom, do you think I could write a book someday?

Rachel smiled. Of course you can. If you have a story to tell, the world is waiting to hear it.

Eventually, Rachel decided to leave teaching and focus entirely on her writing and speaking career. She traveled across the country, sharing her journey with educators, students, and parents. Her talks often ended with a simple message:

Sometimes life doesn't unfold the way we expect, but asking yourself 'why' you're doing what you are doing can be the crucial first step in your journey. Every

detour and challenge offers an opportunity to reflect, learn, and pivot. It is in these moments of questioning that you can rediscover yourself, embrace new passions and find a path that feels more aligned with your true purpose.

Through her writing, Rachel not only rediscovered her own passion but also inspired countless others to do the same.

Rachel's first speaking engagement came shortly after her book was published. It was an invitation to speak at a local teachers' conference. The thought of standing before an audience of hundreds of educators, many of whom had years more experience than her, was intimidating. But the more she thought about it, the more she realized that her authenticity was her greatest strength. She was not there to lecture or give a perfect presentation; she was there to share her journey, her failures, and what she had learned along the way.

When the day came, Rachel stood at the podium, feeling a mixture of excitement and nervousness. She began by telling the story of how she ended up in teaching, not by choice, but by necessity. She shared the highs and lows, the overwhelming demands of the job, and the moments of self-doubt.

Her honesty struck a chord. Teachers in the audience nodded in recognition, many of them silently acknowledging the same struggles in their own lives. Rachel encouraged them to take time for themselves, to rediscover their passions, and to remember that their work was important no matter how unseen or unappreciated it sometimes felt.

By the end of the session, she received a standing ovation, a moment that left her in awe. It was the first time she realized how much her voice mattered to others.

As word spread about Rachel's speech, more invitations came in. She began speaking at school workshops, national conferences, and even webinars for international education groups. Each engagement offered a new opportunity to connect with teachers and parents who were grappling with the same issues she had faced: burnout, lack of support, and the pressure to be everything for everyone.

Her speeches were never about offering a quick fix or pretending that everything could be solved with a few simple strategies. Instead, Rachel focused on real, actionable advice:

Setting Boundaries: She talked about the importance of saying no and recognizing that self-care was not a luxury, but a necessity.

Rediscovering Passion: She encouraged educators to take time away from their classrooms to reconnect with their 'why' and remember what had drawn them to teaching in the first place.

Building a Support System: Rachel emphasized the need for teachers to lean on one another, creating

networks of support where they could share experiences and advice without judgment.

Each speech ended with Rachel's trademark honesty: *It's okay to not have it all figured out. I certainly didn't. But I kept going, one step at a time, and found a way to make this work for me.'*

Asking yourself *why* you feel stuck or unfulfilled is often the starting point of rediscovering your purpose. Why do your goals matter to you? Understanding the deeper reasons behind your actions can lead to greater fulfillment and a clearer sense of direction.

For Rachel, this question came to life during her speaking career, where she truly connected with her audience. After every speech, she took time to listen to others' stories especially the teachers who felt stuck, lost in a career that once brought them joy but now drained them. One of the most memorable encounters was with a middle-aged teacher who admitted to feeling invisible, her passion for teaching diminished by the weight of the job.

Rachel responded by reminding her, you are not failing. You are human. It's okay to need help, and it's okay to admit that you're struggling. This conversation served as a powerful reminder that rediscovering one's purpose is not about perfection, but about acknowledging the *why* behind what we do and embracing the journey to fulfillment. It's about reconnecting with what drives us, whether that's passion for teaching, for creativity, or for something else entirely.

Rachel's own journey from teacher to author and speaker was a testament to this process of asking *why*.

She found fulfillment not from external success, but from embracing her authentic self. By sharing her struggles, she not only empowered others to find their own paths to fulfillment but also gave them permission to admit their challenges. Through vulnerability, she helped others discover their true purpose and reclaim their joy.

Chapter 2: WHAT: Define Your Goals

The trouble with not having a goal is that you can spend your life running up and down the field and never score.'

– Bill Copeland

Imagine standing in the heart of the vast Masai Mara in Kenya. You have decided to explore this iconic park in your great safari car, excited by the promise of golden savannas, grazing wildebeest, and prowling lions.

At first, the journey feels exhilarating, the open expanse beckoning you forward. But soon, you find yourself at a crossroads with no clear signposts. Every direction looks the same with endless plains stretching as far as the eye can see. The excitement gives way to uncertainty. Where do you go next?

Without a map or a specific destination in mind, the freedom of exploration becomes overwhelming. You

could wander aimlessly, burning fuel and time, unsure if you are heading toward the river where the hippos bathe or away from the hidden beauty of the forested hills. But with a well-marked map and a clear goal and perhaps the Mara River crossing or the sunrise view from Ole Opoli lookout hill every turn gains purpose and every mile brings you closer to something extraordinary.

Setting goals in life is just like navigating the Masai Mara. Without defined objectives, it's easy to feel lost, even when the opportunities seem boundless. But with

clarity and direction, the vastness becomes manageable, and every step moves you toward a destination worth reaching.

In this chapter, we look at the guide that defines your goals with the precision of planning a safari adventure. You will learn how to identify your own Mara River, the

place where you feel the magic and know you have arrived. It is time to plot your course and start the journey with confidence.

Let's focus on one area that most of us know: improving our health. It is something many of us want, but without defining what we mean by 'healthy,' the goal remains vague and progress feels out of reach.

For example, you might tell yourself, I want to be healthier. But what does that really mean? Do you want to lose weight? Sleep better? Feel less stressed? Have

more energy? Without clarity, it's like driving aimlessly in the vast Masai Mara. You are moving but you are not sure where you are heading to.

To define your what, start by being specific. Instead of saying, I want to be healthier, you might decide:

I want to lose 10 pounds in the next three months.

I want to walk 10,000 steps every day.

I want to reduce my sugar intake to no more than 25 grams per day.

I want to sleep at least 7 hours every night.

These specific goals take the abstract idea of 'health' and turn it into something measurable and actionable.

When you define your goals, you create a clear destination. Imagine you want to lose 10 pounds. That goal becomes your focus and you can then work backward to figure out how to get there. You might break it down into smaller steps, like:

Meal prepping healthy lunches for the week.

Drinking more water' maybe a goal of eight glasses a day.

Setting aside 30 minutes for exercise, five days a week.

Each small action becomes a step toward your 'what'

Now imagine the alternative. You just say, I want to be healthier. Without a specific goal, it is hard to track progress or stay motivated. One day you might eat a salad and feel good, but the next, you skip a workout and feel like you are failing because you never defined what success looks like in the first place.

Defining your what also helps you connect it to your why. Why do you want to improve your health? Is it to have more energy to play with your kids? To feel more confident? To reduce the risk of illness? When your goals are tied to a purpose that matters to you, they become more motivating.

For instance, if your 'why' is to feel energized for your family, you might decide: My goal is to take a 30-minute walk every morning so I can start my day feeling fresh and ready to tackle family activities. This goal is specific, actionable and meaningful.

A Clear 'What' Keeps You Focused

Life gets busy, and distractions are everywhere. But when you have a clear what, it's easier to stay on track. Let us say you are tempted by a late-night Netflix marathon. Instead of staying up and feeling groggy the next day, your clear goal of getting 7 hours of sleep reminds you to turn off Netflix and head to bed.

Defining your goals does not mean being rigid. It means giving yourself a destination and the tools to get there. And the beauty is, once you reach one goal, you can define a new what and keep moving forward.

So, take a moment now. What does 'healthy' mean to you? Write it down. Be as specific as possible. This is your first step toward a healthier, more focused life.

Take Rose, for example. She wanted to focus on her health but did not want to give up the little things that made her life enjoyable. Instead of going for an extreme overhaul, she decided to define her goals in a way that worked for her lifestyle which was sustainable and enjoyable, while still moving her closer to her 'what'

Rose's 'what' was clear: she wanted to feel more energized, improve her fitness and maintain her weight while still enjoying her favorite foods. Her routine became a mix of small, realistic changes that she could stick to every day.

Rose began her mornings with a simple ritual: a glass of warm water with lemon. This refreshing start helped her hydrate and detoxify her body. Afterward, she rewarded herself with her favorite cup of coffee because giving it up was not part of her plan.

Breakfast was important to Rose, and she did not believe in skipping it. She loved her morning toast with an egg and she wasn't about to give up wheat entirely. On some mornings, she switched it up with a warm bowl of oats porridge. Both options gave her the energy she needed to start her day.

Rose made sure to eat at least one piece of fruit daily. Whether it was an apple, a handful of berries, or both, she ensured her body got the nutrients it needed in a simple, delicious way.

Throughout the day, Rose drank plenty of water but added a little twist to make it more interesting. Sometimes she infused her water with lemon slices, cucumber, or chia seeds. These small additions made staying hydrated feel refreshing and fun. She also ensured she carried her bottler everywhere she went to have little sips of water as she could never have a full glass of water.

Rose committed to eating a portion of vegetables every day. It did not have to be fancy, sometimes it was a simple salad or steamed veggies. She also decided not to eat carbs after 6:30 PM, which helped her feel lighter and sleep better at night.

Sleep became non-negotiable for Rose. She aimed for at least 7 hours of rest each night, knowing that proper sleep was just as important as her diet and exercise.

Rose's exercise routine was refreshingly simple and easy to fit into her day:

Living on the 5th floor of her apartment building, Rose decided to skip the lift entirely. Climbing the stairs became her primary workout, and she loved how it got her heart pumping without taking extra time out of her day.

Inside her home, Rose found creative ways to stay active. She did a few squats while brushing her teeth, turned on her favorite songs and danced in front of the TV, and stretched during commercial breaks. These little bursts of activity added up and kept her moving without feeling like a chore.

Rose's approach worked because it was not about strict rules or deprivation. It was about balance and making small, intentional choices that aligned with her 'what'. She still enjoyed her favorite toast and coffee, even a chapati (similar to naan bread} but she balanced it with nutritious habits like eating fruits, staying hydrated, and moving her body daily.

By defining her goals and sticking to a routine that suited her life, Rose not only felt healthier and more energetic but also more confident in her ability to make positive changes. Her 'what' to feel energized and fit was not just a distant dream anymore; it was something she lived every day, one step (and one lemon-water) at a time.

What about you? What small, simple steps can you take to define and move toward your what? Like Rose, you can find a balance that works for you, making the journey to better health both enjoyable and achievable.

Every goal comes with challenges. Recognizing this can help you prepare for them.

Rose's Obstacles: For Rose, life was not always predictable. Some days were so busy she could not climb the stairs or cook a balanced meal. On those

days, she did not beat herself up. Instead, she reminded herself that every effort counts and focused on doing better the next day. For late-night cravings, she kept healthy snacks like nuts or yogurt ready to satisfy her hunger without guilt.

Think about the obstacles you might face. Busy days? Unexpected cravings? Lack of motivation? Prepare simple solutions in advance, such as keeping a fruit bowl on your desk, setting alarms to remind you to drink water, using a smartwatch that reminds you it's time to move or pre-planning meals for the week.

Tracking your progress is a great way to stay motivated and see how far you have come.

Rose kept it simple. She used a notebook to jot down her daily habits, like climbing the stairs, drinking her water, or getting her 7 hours of sleep. Seeing those little check marks at the end of the day gave her a sense of accomplishment.

Use a journal, an app, or even sticky notes to track your daily habits. Celebrate your consistency; it's not just about the destination but also about the journey.

Small wins build momentum and confidence. Every step forward is worth celebrating.

When Rose achieved small milestones, like sticking to her lemon-water routine for a week or reaching her hydration goal every day, she treated herself to something special; a relaxing bath or her favorite book.

What can you reward yourself with when you reach a milestone? It doesn't have to be expensive or elaborate. Treat yourself to something that makes you smile and reinforces your progress.

Mindfulness enhances your connection to your goals and makes the process more enjoyable.

Rose practiced mindfulness by paying attention to her choices. She savored her morning coffee, took a moment to appreciate the crisp taste of her infused water, and noticed how energized she felt after climbing the stairs.

Pause to reflect on how your actions align with your what. Enjoy your meals without distractions, take deep breaths during exercise, and appreciate how far you have come.

Remember that goals are not set in stone, they are meant to evolve with you.

Over time, Rose's goals shifted. Once she became consistent with her routine, she added new goals, like trying yoga, experimenting with new vegetables in her meals. Don't be afraid to review and adjust your goals. Maybe life gets busier, or you realize you want to focus on a different area of health. Adapt your what to fit your current reality.

Sometimes, it's easier to stick to your goals with support from others. Rose found a dedicated walking area where many people went for walks. She did it with

her buddy who was her neighbour. They also started climbing the stairs up and down together, turning it into a fun and encouraging activity for 10 minutes each day.

Share your goals with a friend, join an online group, or look for a local class. Support and encouragement can make all the difference.

To help define your what, try this simple exercise:

Close your eyes and imagine yourself as the healthiest version of you. What does your day look like? How do you feel? What habits make you proud?

Write down what comes to mind.

This exercise connects you emotionally to your goals and makes them feel more tangible.

Rose's journey is a reminder that defining your what does not have to be overwhelming. It's about making small, intentional choices that align with what matters to you. Whether it's sipping lemon water in the morning, taking the stairs, or savoring your favorite breakfast, every step brings you closer to your goal.

Your 'what' is waiting for you to define it. What will yours be? Take that first step today because every journey begins with a clear destination.

Chapter 3: WHERE: Create the Right Environment

'To each, there comes in their lifetime a special moment when they are figuratively tapped on the shoulder and offered the chance to do a very special thing, unique to their talents and circumstances.'

- Winston Churchill

Where you are, whether it is physically, mentally or emotionally plays a crucial role in whether you thrive or merely survive. Ask yourself: Is my current environment serving me, or is it holding me back? And more importantly 'where' do I need to be to thrive?

Rachel's story illustrates how the right environment or the lack of it can shape not just your career but your entire sense of self.

Rachel had spent over a decade living her dream, contributing to impactful humanitarian projects through her work with the United Nations. She was confident,

purposeful and fulfilled. However, when circumstances forced her into teaching, her new environment came with challenges she was not prepared for.

Physically her long hours in a demanding school setting left Rachel exhausted. Her weekends were often consumed by extracurricular responsibilities and even her home didn't feel like a sanctuary, as grading and planning followed her there.

Mentally, Rachel felt stuck. She struggled to reconcile her new reality with the career she had envisioned for herself. The constant pressure to meet high expectations, both academically and socially, drained her. Also emotionally the stress of managing students, parents and her own children left Rachel feeling disconnected from herself and her family. She often questioned if this life was sustainable

and whether it aligned with her core values and long-term goals.

To flourish, you must take stock of your current environment and imagine what a healthier, more

fulfilling version of that environment looks like. For Rachel, it meant asking herself critical questions such as

What kind of work energizes me rather than depletes me?

How can I create boundaries to protect my time and peace of mind?

What changes can I make to feel more aligned with my values and passions?

By identifying where she needed to be physically, mentally and emotionally, Rachel could begin to create a plan to transition out of survival mode and into a successful state.

Some of the steps that you can use to create the right Environment are

Assess Your Current Environment

Take an honest inventory of your physical, mental and emotional space. What is working for you? What feels draining?

For Rachel: She acknowledged that while the job provided financial stability and reduced school fees, the trade-offs were too steep. Her environment did not nurture her creativity, energy or peace of mind.

Clarify Your Needs

What do you need to feel balanced and fulfilled? This could be more time for self-care, better boundaries at

work, or a shift to a career that aligns with your passions.

For Rachel: She realized she needed a job that allowed her to spend more quality time with her children and gave her the freedom to be herself.

Make Gradual Changes

Creating the right environment doesn't always require an immediate overhaul. Start small, focusing on areas you can control. For Rachel: She began setting boundaries, such as limiting her grading time in the evenings and saying no to non-essential extracurricular commitments. She also carved out time for herself, whether it was a quiet walk after work or a game night with her kids.

Seek Support

Sometimes, creating the right environment means leaning on others for guidance and encouragement. For Rachel: She confided in close friends and sought advice from colleagues who had found ways to manage the school's demands without burning out.

Plan for a Transition

If your current environment is not where you want to stay long-term, start planning the steps to transition toward your ideal future. For Rachel, she realized that her teaching career, though rewarding in many ways, was not her long-term vision. Instead of staying stagnant, she began planning her exit strategy: she decided to focus on her passion for writing. Rachel set a clear goal that she would write one chapter a month, building toward her dream of completing a book. This structured approach gave her the clarity she needed, allowing her to gradually move from her current reality to the future she envisioned, where she could combine her love for writing and speaking while embracing a flexible lifestyle.

Creating the right environment is not about finding perfection but it's about designing a space where you can grow, thrive, and feel aligned with your purpose. Rachel's journey serves as a reminder that while circumstances may push us into uncomfortable places, we have the power to redefine where we are and where we want to go. It starts with asking the right questions: Where am I now? Where do I want to be? And what steps will get me there?

Your environment is more than just a physical space; it's the sum of your experiences, mindset and support system. When you align your environment with your goals and values, you set yourself up for true fulfillment. Where do you need to be to thrive? Start creating that space today.

Your environment is not just the physical or external circumstances but it is also the mindset you bring into

it. Sometimes, changing your perspective can be as powerful as changing your surroundings.

Rachel's Perspective Shift: Rachel's perspective shifted as she started to recognize that while teaching was not her ultimate passion, it offered her a wealth of skills and experiences that would be invaluable in her writing journey. Her daily work of researching lesson plans, creating engaging activities, and finding creative ways to explain concepts sparked ideas for her book. Every interaction with her students, every lesson she taught, and every challenge she faced in the classroom served as a lesson in how to approach her writing.

Rather than focusing on the aspects of teaching that drained her, Rachel began to view her job as a stepping stone, teaching her new ways to connect with people, communicate effectively, and think critically. The structure she developed for lesson planning mirrored how she began planning her book, one chapter at a time.

She recognized that her time in the classroom was feeding her creativity and helping her refine her voice as a writer. Every small moment became an opportunity for growth, and instead of resenting her teaching career, Rachel started seeing it as the foundation for her future work as an author.

Your Perspective: Ask yourself, what can I learn from my current environment? How can I reframe challenges as opportunities for growth? Shifting your mindset doesn't mean ignoring problems, but it helps you see possibilities even in difficult situations.

Your immediate physical environment has a profound impact on your mental and emotional well-being. Organizing and personalizing your space can help you feel more in control and motivated. Rachel transformed her home workspace into a place of inspiration. She added plants, motivational quotes, and a vision board of her long-term goals. This helped her feel grounded and reminded her of her aspirations, even during tough days.

Take a moment to assess your environment. Is it cluttered or chaotic? Do you feel inspired when you are in it? Small changes like decluttering, adding natural light, or including personal touches can make a big difference.

A thriving environment is not just about external factors it's also about how you manage stress, setbacks, and emotions. Emotional resilience helps you stay grounded and adapt to challenges. To manage the stress of demanding parents and late nights, Rachel

practiced mindfulness techniques. She started journaling to process her emotions and meditated for 10 minutes before bed to clear her mind.

Your Resilience Plan: Incorporate practices that help you recharge emotionally, whether it's journaling, meditation, spending time in nature, or connecting with

loved ones. Emotional resilience creates an inner environment that supports your goals.

Your relationships are a key part of your environment. Surrounding yourself with people who uplift, inspire, and challenge you positively can significantly impact your journey.

Rachel's Network: Rachel built connections with supportive colleagues who shared her challenges and offered advice. She also reconnected with mentors from her previous career, seeking guidance for her next steps.

Your Connections: Reflect on the people in your life. Are they supportive of your goals, or do they drain your energy? Seek relationships that encourage growth and align with the environment you want to create.

Sometimes, the right environment requires tapping into external resources, such as books, courses or communities, to grow and thrive.

Rachel's Resources: To improve her teaching skills and find new ways to manage her classroom, Rachel enrolled in online workshops and joined a professional network for educators. She found that these resources provided not only teaching strategies but also the emotional support needed to handle the daily pressures of being a teacher. Additionally, she read books on work-life balance and personal growth, which helped her navigate her challenges and maintain a healthier perspective on her profession.

But Rachel did not stop there, she also turned to her colleagues for guidance. By observing how other teachers in her school managed their classrooms, she discovered various techniques that helped them stay organized, engaged and positive.

She paid close attention to their approaches; some teachers excelled at keeping students focused during group work, while others had a talent for making lessons feel interactive and fun. Watching how they communicated with students, handled disruptions and balanced workloads gave Rachel valuable insights into her own teaching style.

These observations allowed Rachel to refine her approach, combining the strategies she had learned in workshops with the real-world practices she saw from her peers. In doing so, she became more efficient, confident, and better equipped to manage her class.

This not only improved her teaching skills but also provided her with the tools and inspiration needed to pursue her writing goals with renewed focus and determination.

Your Toolkit: Consider what resources you need to build your ideal environment. These could include online courses, mentorship programs or even apps that help you stay organized and motivated.

The right environment is one that energizes you rather than drains you. Pay attention to where your energy goes and how you can manage it better.

Rachel's Energy Audit: Rachel's Energy Audit: As Rachel continued to manage her busy teaching schedule, she realized that overcommitting to extracurricular activities and taking on too many responsibilities outside of class was slowly draining her energy. She found herself overwhelmed with lesson planning, grading, and trying to balance everything at home. To regain her sense of control and make more time for her personal goals, she started conducting an energy audit. This meant carefully evaluating her commitments and prioritizing tasks that aligned with her strengths and passions.

One of the key steps in her energy audit was learning to delegate where possible. For example, Rachel found that she could hand over certain responsibilities to her students, such as having them help with organizing class materials or running some of the smaller group activities. This allowed her to focus on what mattered most: creating an engaging and effective learning environment.

Rachel also discovered the power of using online tools to streamline her lesson planning. She had always spent hours crafting intricate lesson plans, but after learning about several user-friendly educational websites, she began using templates and resources that made the process quicker and less time-consuming. Tools like Google Classroom, Canva for Education, and lesson-planning apps allowed her to create and organize materials more efficiently. These platforms provided ready-made templates for various subjects and grade levels, enabling her to customize content quickly rather than starting from scratch every time.

By using these tools, Rachel could plan more effectively and save valuable time, which she could then devote to other tasks such as reading, writing or spending time with her family. This shift in mindset allowed Rachel to regain her energy and focus on what truly mattered to her, both in her teaching and in her personal life.

Your Energy Plan: Take an energy audit of your daily life. What activities or environments leave you feeling refreshed? Which ones leave you exhausted? Adjust your schedule and commitments to focus on what truly matters.

Finally, take the time to envision your ideal environment. What does it look like, feel like, and offer

you? Write it down or create a vision board to make it tangible.

Rachel's Vision: Rachel envisioned a life where she felt fulfilled, balanced and connected to her family. Her ideal environment included meaningful work that aligned with her passions, time for personal growth, and a supportive community. This vision guided her decisions moving forward.

Your Vision: Imagine your thriving environment. What changes do you need to make to get closer to that vision? Use this as a roadmap to guide your journey.

Creating the right environment is not a one-time task; it's an ongoing process of aligning your physical, mental, and emotional space with your goals and values. As Rachel's story shows, even when life throws you unexpected challenges, you have the power to redefine where you are and create a space that allows you to thrive.

Ask yourself: What environment will help me succeed? How can I start creating it today? Your future self will thank you.

Chapter 4: WHEN: Take Action at the Right Time

'The secret of getting ahead is getting started.' – Mark Twain

Timing is everything. It's the subtle difference between planting seeds in the spring, when the soil is fertile and ready, and trying to force growth in the cold, barren ground of winter. In life, knowing when to act can shape the outcomes of your decisions.

But how do you know when it's the right time to make a change? How do you differentiate between waiting for the right moment and procrastinating out of fear or uncertainty?

Recognizing Procrastination

Often, we delay taking action because we are afraid of failure or overwhelmed by the unknown. Procrastination is not just about putting things off, it's about the internal barriers that stop us from starting.

Take the story of Daniel, a 42-year-old IT specialist who had worked at the same company for 18 years. Daniel had always been passionate about technology and dreamt of launching his own business. However, he kept putting it off. He'd tell himself, I will wait until I have more savings, or Maybe next year, when the timing is better.

That all changed when the COVID-19 pandemic hit. The company where Daniel worked shifted to remote work, and soon after, Daniel's role was made redundant due to financial constraints and company restructuring. At 42, with no backup plan in place, Daniel found himself suddenly unemployed.

At first, Daniel was in shock. His job had been a stable part of his life for almost two decades. But as weeks passed, he realized that being at home full-time gave him an unexpected opportunity: the chance to finally focus on the business idea he had always dreamed about.

During the lockdown, Daniel had spent more time than ever online, researching trends in e-commerce, remote work solutions, and digital tools. He began to recognize a growing need in the market for digital transformation services, especially for small businesses struggling to pivot to an online presence during the pandemic.

That's when Daniel decided to act. With his background in IT and a strong understanding of technology, he launched an online consultancy called TechBridge Solutions. His company would help small businesses transition to digital platforms by setting up websites, integrating e-commerce solutions, and teaching them how to navigate remote work tools.

Daniel knew that starting his own business would not be easy, especially in the middle of a global crisis. However, he was determined to take this opportunity seriously. The first step was creating a timeline:

First month: He built a website for TechBridge Solutions, showcasing his services and skills.

Second month: He started to reach out to potential clients through social media, online ads, and networking.

Third month: Secure at least three clients and offer them packages for digital setup.

Sixth month: Start offering digital workshops on platforms like Zoom, teaching small businesses how to use tools like Google Workspace, Zoom, and Shopify.

Daniel broke his goal into manageable steps, with clear deadlines to keep himself accountable. Each month, he checked off milestones, and the confidence built with every small success.

One of the hardest lessons for Daniel was learning patience. The first few months of his business were slow. Though he had secured a few clients, the income was not steady. Some weeks, it felt like he was getting nowhere, and the worry started to creep in.

But Daniel reminded himself that building a business takes time especially when you are starting from scratch and in the thick of a pandemic. He chose to focus on long-term growth, rather than expecting instant results.

As his business started to grow, Daniel celebrated small wins like getting positive feedback from his clients or successfully launching an e-commerce platform for a local bakery. These little milestones helped keep him motivated during the inevitable challenges.

So how did Daniel recognize the right time to act?

It was not just the external circumstances, like the COVID-19 pandemic, that served as a wake-up call for Daniel. He had been contemplating starting a business for years, but the pandemic created the perfect storm of opportunity and necessity. It pushed him to realize that if he did not act now, he might regret it forever.

For Daniel, the right time came when he had reached his breaking point with procrastination. Instead of waiting for the 'perfect' moment to start his business, he chose to start now with the resources available. He realized that the longer he waited, the more likely he would stay stuck in the same place.

As with any new business, Daniel faced his share of challenges. Some clients were slow to respond; others were hesitant about moving their businesses online. There were days when he wondered if he had made the right decision.

But Daniel kept pushing forward. He continued to learn new skills which included attending online webinars about digital marketing, improving his website design skills, and learning about SEO to drive traffic. He focused on the clients he had and made sure to offer them exceptional service.

He also focused on building relationships. Through consistent communication and high-quality service, he gained loyal clients who referred him to others. Over time, his business grew, and what started as a necessity during uncertain times became a thriving venture.

Your 'When'

Daniel's story highlights an essential truth: the right time to act is rarely obvious or convenient. It often comes disguised as a challenge or a moment of discomfort. But with the right mindset and strategies, you can turn those moments into opportunities.

Here's how to find your 'when'

Acknowledge Procrastination: Identify whether your hesitation is rooted in fear or genuine un-readiness.

Define Your Opportunity: Look for the gaps or needs around you that align with your strengths.

Take the First Step: Do not wait for a perfect plan; start with what you have.

Stay Patient: Understand that results take time and effort.

The right time to make a change is often now. The circumstances may not be ideal, but the willingness to act and adapt is what sets successful individuals apart. Like Daniel, you can create your own opportunities even in the face of challenges by taking that crucial first step and trusting the process.

Remember: Life does not wait, so why should you?

Chapter 5: WHO: Build Your Support System

'Surround yourself with only people who are going to lift you higher.' – Oprah Winfrey

Success is rarely a solo journey. Behind every thriving individual is a network of people who uplift, guide, and inspire them. To achieve your goals, it is crucial to identify who you need in your life, how to nurture those relationships, and when to let go of connections that no longer serve you.

Who Do You Need in Your Life to Help You Succeed?

No matter how self-reliant you are, there are moments when having the right people around you can make all the difference. A solid support system can include:

Mentors

Mentors are individuals who offer invaluable insight and guidance, especially when you are navigating new or challenging territory. Rachel, for example, recognized the power of mentorship when she set her sights on writing her book. She joined online author groups to learn from experienced writers who had walked the

same path. These groups provided a wealth of knowledge about writing, publishing, and overcoming writer's block, helping her stay on track with her manuscript.

In addition to these online resources, Rachel also turned to her old connections at the United Nations. Several former colleagues who had been part of various projects offered advice and perspective on her manuscript. They not only shared practical tips but also helped her refine her approach, offering feedback that made her work stronger.

Like a good mentor, these individuals did not just provide the answers, they challenged Rachel to think differently, broadened her perspective, and encouraged her to step outside her comfort zone. Their advice pushed her to approach her book with a clearer vision and confidence, showing the true power of mentorship in any field.

Accountability Partners

Accountability partners are those individuals who help keep us on track, ensuring that we follow through on the goals we set and celebrating our progress along the way. For Rachel, this support came from both within her school and through online networks, where she found peers who were also navigating similar journeys.

At her school, Rachel's closest accountability partner was a fellow teacher, Gladys, who had started her own side project of creating educational resources while still managing her full-time teaching responsibilities. Gladys understood the struggles of balancing multiple roles

and was a constant source of motivation. They would often check in with each other, setting small, achievable goals such as completing a chapter draft or finalizing a lesson plan and celebrating when these were met.

When Rachel felt overwhelmed with her teaching duties, Gladys would remind her of the progress she had made, keeping her focused on the bigger picture.

Rachel also connected with a group of like-minded educators through an online writing community. Many of these teachers were in similar positions struggling to find time to write while balancing full teaching workloads. They set up regular virtual check-ins where they would share their progress, ask for advice, and provide feedback on each other's writing. The group helped Rachel stay disciplined, offering encouragement when things felt tough and providing valuable feedback when she needed direction.

Through these accountability partners both near and far, Rachel found the support and encouragement she needed to stay on track with her goals. These partnerships were not just about checking off tasks; they were about mutual understanding, empathy, and celebrating progress together.

Whether it was Gladys's reassuring words or the collective support from her online writing group, Rachel was reminded that she wasn't alone in her journey and that made all the difference in keeping her moving forward.

Cheerleaders

Everyone needs cheerleaders may they be friends or family who steadfastly believe in you, especially during moments of self-doubt. These are the people who remind you of your purpose, your potential, and the reasons you started in the first place. For Rachel, her biggest cheerleaders were her children, especially her eldest, Sean.

Sean, at an age where he could understand the dedication his mom was putting into her writing, became her loudest supporter. He would often sit with her during her writing sessions, offering suggestions or just keeping her company. On particularly tough days when Rachel felt stuck or unsure, Sean would gently

remind her, 'Mom, remember how you always say stories matter? Yours does too.

Rachel found Sean's enthusiasm infectious. He would ask about her progress, express excitement about her ideas, and even boast to his friends at school about the book his mom was writing. His genuine pride in her efforts was a powerful motivator, pushing Rachel to keep going even when the path felt uphill.

Her younger child Kiki, while not fully understanding the depth of her work, would cheer Rachel on in their own way, through hugs and little notes of

encouragement. Together, her children brought a lightness and energy that reminded Rachel of her 'why' she was not just writing for herself but to inspire, for her kids, and for others who needed her voice.

In addition to her children, Rachel's broader circle of cheerleaders included friends and former colleagues who regularly checked in and celebrated her milestones. These individuals, just like her kids, played a critical role in keeping her spirits high, serving as constant reminders that her journey was worth every ounce of effort.

Collaborators

Sometimes, success requires teamwork. Collaborators bring skills and perspectives that complement your own, helping you achieve what might feel impossible alone. For Rachel, this became evident as she worked

on her book while balancing her responsibilities as a teacher and mother.

Within her school, fellow teachers played a pivotal role. When Rachel shared her aspirations to write a book, some of her colleagues eagerly supported her journey.

One teacher, Ms. Diana, known for her organizational skills, offered tips on structuring ideas effectively insights that Rachel used to outline her chapters. Mr. Ouma, who was an avid reader, provided valuable feedback on early drafts, pointing out areas where the narrative could be more engaging or impactful. These interactions gave Rachel a sense of community and encouragement, reminding her she wasn't working in isolation.

Online, Rachel connected with a network of aspiring and established authors. She joined forums on TikTok Authors and also participated in virtual writing workshops, where writers would exchange ideas, critique each other's work, and share strategies for overcoming common challenges like writer's block or

time management. Through these platforms, Rachel learned about tools and resources that streamlined the writing process, from outlining software to self-publishing platforms.

Her collaborators extended beyond the writing community. Rachel reached out to her former colleagues at the United Nations, many of whom had experience with publication. One of them, Steve, a seasoned editor, reviewed her manuscript and offered professional advice on how to polish it for her intended audience. Another colleague shared insights about making the content relatable and universal, drawing

from their shared experiences in global humanitarian work.

Together, these collaborators enriched Rachel's writing journey, bringing expertise, encouragement and diverse perspectives. They demonstrated the power of teamwork and reinforced the idea that collaboration is a cornerstone of success.

Experts

Whether it's a coach, therapist, financial advisor, or teacher, seeking professional help in specific areas can fast-track your growth. Experts provide actionable strategies and specialized knowledge to guide your journey. For Rachel, this was particularly true in her path to becoming a published author.

After completing her manuscript, Rachel decided to work with a professional publisher. The publisher not only reviewed her manuscript but also provided invaluable feedback. They highlighted areas where the narrative could be refined, suggested tweaks to improve flow, and gave her insights into what makes a book resonate with readers. This guidance elevated her work, helping her produce a manuscript that was both polished and impactful.

In addition to professional publishing advice, Rachel explored self-publishing platforms like Amazon KDP (Kindle Direct Publishing). While initially overwhelming, she dedicated time to learning how to navigate the platform. She researched topics like formatting, cover design, and marketing strategies. Rachel joined online forums where independent authors shared tips about pricing, maximizing visibility, and leveraging keywords to ensure her book reached the right audience.

Through these resources, she discovered practical tools, such as templates for formatting and promotional tools provided by Amazon KDP, that made the self-publishing process manageable. This journey not only gave her confidence in launching her book but also opened new avenues for sharing her work widely.

By seeking out experts and leveraging specialized platforms, Rachel turned what seemed like a daunting dream into a structured, actionable reality. Their insights empowered her to make informed decisions and ensured her book's success in an increasingly competitive market.

Fostering Meaningful Relationships

Once you identify who you need in your support system, the next step is to build and maintain those relationships. Here are some tips:

Be Genuine

Authenticity is the foundation of any meaningful relationship. Be honest about your goals, challenges, and the kind of support you need.

Give and Take

Strong relationships are reciprocal. Offer your time, skills, or support in return. When others see you investing in their success, they will be more inclined to invest in yours.

Communicate Clearly

Whether it's sharing your goals with a mentor or discussing boundaries with a friend, clear communication is key. Misunderstandings can strain even the strongest relationships.

Show Gratitude

A simple 'thank you' goes a long way. Acknowledge the contributions of those in your support system, and let them know they're appreciated.

Letting Go of Toxic Connections

While building your support system, you may encounter people who drain your energy, discourage your goals, or hold you back. Letting go of toxic relationships can be challenging but necessary.

Signs of Toxic Connections

Constant negativity or criticism.

Lack of support for your goals.

Manipulation, guilt-tripping, or other forms of emotional abuse.

Jealousy or competition instead of collaboration.

How to Let Go

Set Boundaries: Politely but firmly communicate your limits.

Gradually Distance Yourself: Spend less time engaging with them.

Focus on Healthy Relationships: Replace toxic connections with positive ones.

Finding the Right People for Your Journey

If you are unsure where to start, here are some suggestions:

Networking: Attend events, join groups, or participate in online communities related to your goals.

Reconnecting: Reach out to old friends or colleagues who might share your vision.

Seeking Help: Do not hesitate to approach professionals or mentors you admire.

Building a support system is not about surrounding yourself with as many people as possible but it is about finding the right people.

Meaningful relationships are a two-way street. Give as much as you receive.

Letting go of toxic connections creates space for healthier ones to thrive.

Success isn't just about what you know, it's also about who you know and how they contribute to your journey.

Your support system is your safety net, your sounding board, and your motivator. Surround yourself with

people who align with your goals, share your values, and inspire you to keep moving forward. The journey

may be yours alone, but with the right people by your side, it becomes infinitely richer and more rewarding.

Conclusion: Embrace the Journey of Transformation

As you close this book, pause for a moment to reflect on the powerful journey you have embarked upon. You have explored the essential 5 W's; Why, What, Where, When, and Who with each explaining a crucial piece in the puzzle of personal transformation. These questions are not just tools for change; they are your lifelong companions, guiding you through the evolving chapters of your life.

Your 'Why' is the foundation. It holds the key to unlocking your deepest motivations and desires. Understanding why you feel stuck or unfulfilled is the first step in breaking free from the limitations that hold you back. Keep digging into your why, as it will continue to evolve with your experiences and growth.

The 'What' is the vision you create for yourself. Defining your goals with clarity allows you to chart a path forward. Goals are not static but they are dynamic

and ever changing as you learn more about yourself and the world. Don't fear failure; it's simply a step toward success. Use the strategies in this book to overcome doubts, refine your objectives, and move closer to the life you truly want.

Your 'Where' matters. It's not just about your physical surroundings but also your mental and emotional environment. Ask yourself regularly: Is this space, relationship, or mindset helping me thrive? If not, have the courage to make adjustments. Building an environment that supports your growth is an ongoing process, and it requires you to be intentional about where you choose to place your energy.

Timing is everything, and that's where the 'When' comes in. Change cannot always happen overnight, but neither should you let procrastination hold you back. Recognize when it's time to act and when patience is required. The balance between urgency and readiness is delicate, but by following the strategies outlined in this book, you can develop the ability to seize the right opportunities while allowing space for natural growth.

Never underestimate the power of the 'Who' in your life. The people you surround yourself with can elevate or hinder your progress. Cultivating meaningful relationships, finding mentors, and building a support system aligned with your goals will amplify your success. Equally important is the courage to let go of toxic connections and embrace people who genuinely celebrate your growth.

Transformation is not a one-time event; it is an ongoing journey. The 5 W's are not meant to be checked off and forgotten but revisited as often as you need them. Life will continually challenge you, offering opportunities for reflection and growth. When you feel lost, stuck, or uncertain, return to these questions—they will guide you back to clarity and purpose.

As you step forward into your new chapter, remember that progress, not perfection, is what matters. Celebrate the small victories, learn from setbacks, and remain open to the endless possibilities ahead. The answers you seek are already within you, waiting to be uncovered. Trust yourself, and trust the process.

Life is a series of transformations, each bringing you closer to the person you are meant to become. This is your story to write, your journey to own, and your life to live fully.

Go forward boldly, with curiosity and confidence. The journey of transformation is not just a destination but it's a way of living. And the best part? It's only just beginning.

www.ingramcontent.com/pod-product-compliance
Lightning Source LLC
LaVergne TN
LVHW040955150826
845672LV00002B/707

* 9 7 9 8 2 3 0 9 0 3 3 9 0 *